## Day 1

# *Dolly Mixture*

Dolly Mixture is made up of all different shapes and colours, yet they are all made from the same ingredients.

Isn't that like us as human beings? We are all shapes and colours yet all made the same way! God made us in His own image and no matter what our shape or colour He loves us equally.

Our fellowships and churches are like a 'bag of assorted sweets' – all the same in one way, but full of different characters and personalities, skills and gifts, with lots to offer one another.

GW00393046

**Romans 12 verses 4 and 5**

*"Just as each of us has one body with many members, and these members do not all have the same function, so in Christ we who are many form one body, and each member belongs to all the others"*

# Smarties

When I think of these sweets they remind me of my childhood. I used to love being given the little cardboard tube, popping the cap off the end and finding all those brightly coloured sugar coated chocolates. My favourite was the orange one – it always seemed to taste better than the others!

Another sweet memory of my childhood was that I went to Sunday School, and it was there that I heard that Jesus loved me. I am so thankful He does. We need to tell our children that He loves them too. Children are important and precious to Him, so much so that He told the Disciples to let the children come to Him, when they tried to keep them away.

Do you bring the children in your family to the Lord in prayer each day?

---

**Matthew 19 verse 14**

*Jesus said, "Let the little children come to me, and do not hinder them, for the kingdom of heaven belongs to such as these."*

# Day 3

## Fruit Gums

These are chewy, mouth-watering little sweets and are really refreshing. They are flavoured with orange, lemon, strawberry, lime and blackcurrant – all sorts of fruits.

The Bible tells us we need to have the 'fruits' of the Spirit of God apparent in our daily lives. What are the 'fruits' of the Spirit?

They are characteristics which will be evident if we have the Lord in our hearts – Love, Joy, Peace, Patience, Kindness, Goodness, Faithfulness, Gentleness and Self-Control.

How many of these are we displaying in our behaviour and attitudes to those around us?

### Galatians 5 verses 22-24

*"But the fruit of the Spirit is love, joy, peace, patience, kindness, goodness, faithfulness, gentleness and self-control. Against such things there is no law. Those who belong to Jesus Christ have crucified the sinful nature with its passions and desires."*

# Opal Fruits

It's strange how we remember trivial things so well, yet important things slip our minds! I clearly remember the TV advertisement for these sweets!

It had a catchy little tune and went "Opal fruits – made to make your mouth water" and they certainly did that!

The trouble was, after two or three you would really need a drink of water – a bit of a contradiction really.

On one occasion when Jesus was travelling, He became very tired and thirsty. He sat by a well and a woman came to draw water. As they got talking He told her that she wasn't living right and that she would never find what she was really looking for unless she turned to Him and took the 'living water'- or the life He could give.

Are you 'thirsty' for something more in your life? Then why not try Jesus?

**Psalm 42 verse 1**

*"As the deer pants for streams of water,
so my soul longs for you, O God."*

# *Barley Sugar*

Barley Sugar was often given to us as children if we got travel sick, it seemed to have a calming effect on an upset stomach. They are hard-boiled sweets and had to be sucked slowly to feel the benefit!

Sometimes we get all upset and 'bent out of shape' over things and all it needs is for us to sit down for a short while, take it easy and read a Psalm or a verse from God's Word, the Bible, and it can make all the difference – it has a calming effect.

Most of the time if we get around to reading our Bibles, it's all done in a bit of a hurry because we are always so busy – yet the days would probably go so much better if only we would take time to talk to the Lord and read His Word – the answers to all our needs are there!

**Psalm 119 verse 105**

*"Your Word is a lamp to my feet and a light for my path."*

# *Sherbet Lemons*

Sherbet lemons are interesting sweets. You suck the sweets for a while then suddenly as the shell gets thinner you get a surprise – out of the lemon comes a fizzy powder which can sometimes make your eyes water!

Life is a bit like that – you're going along quite nicely, then suddenly from nowhere something comes to surprise or shock you – and it makes your eyes water – with tears!

But do you know that there are no surprises with God? He sees everything, knows when and what will happen, and nothing comes to us – His precious children – except He allows it. It is our reaction to the shocks and surprises in life that matter more to Him. He is always there watching, caring, comforting and supporting us and will bring good out of what seem to be awful things.

---

**Psalm 27 verse 1**

*"The Lord is my light and my salvation – whom shall I fear? The Lord is the stronghold of my life – of whom shall I be afraid?*

# *Liquorice Allsorts*

These are bright, colourful sweets in different shapes and textures, some jelly, some coconut, some fondant but each one of them has one thing in common other than sugar – a dark bitter centre! Some of us eat the sweet bit and leave the centre.

As human beings we are all very different to look at, and can be sweet on the outside, but all with a heart which can be bitter.

Jesus came to enable us to have a change of heart, so that we can be more like Him – sweet all through.

**Isaiah 29 verse 13**

*"The Lord says:*

*These people come near to me with their mouth and honour me with their lips, but their hearts are far from me..."*

# Day 8

## *Jelly Beans*

Some years ago in America, there was a competition to think up a new flavour for a Jelly Bean! These are one of the favourite sweets in the U.S., but they were obviously running out of ideas. They had gone full circle, used every colour and flavour they could think of and were now looking for help, for something new.

Do you feel that you are in a rut maybe, that you have exhausted everything, you have all you need materially, but there is still something missing? Would you like something new and different in your life?

Well, Jesus came to give us the opportunity for a whole new exciting life, if we simply put our trust in Him!

### Psalm 40 verses 2 & 3

*"He lifted me out of the slimy pit, out of the mud and mire; He set my feet on a rock and gave me a firm place to stand. He put a new song in my mouth, a hymn of praise to our God…"*

# Day 9

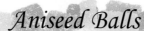

## Aniseed Balls

Aniseed Balls are very hard little sweets with a strong flavour and they take a long time to eat, but the flavour stays right through to the last little bit of the sweet.

Do you have 'staying power'? When things get tough and times are hard, do you give in to anger and frustration and blame God, or do you accept that He never leaves us or abandons us, so you 'hang in there' trusting and waiting for Him to see you through. He always will!

### Psalm 112 verses 1 & 7

*"…Blessed is the man who fears the Lord, who finds great delight in His commands."*

*"He will have no fear of bad news; his heart is steadfast, trusting in the Lord."*

# Humbugs

Humbugs are boiled sweets with a minty flavour and soft chewy centre and are very popular.

However, the meaning of the word 'humbug' in the Dictionary is quite different – it describes a person who is "not sincere or honest".

It's never a nice feeling to discover that someone you like is neither sincere or honest. We are told that God 'detests' lies, so we need always to be honest and reliable. That way we will always have friends and folks will know we can be trusted if we are truthful.

**Proverbs 12 verse 22**

*"The Lord detests lying lips,
but He delights in men who are truthful."*

# Penny Chews

There was a time when we could buy a chewy sweet with a nice raspberry or orange flavour for a penny, and it would last a very long time, it was good value for money. These days a penny goes nowhere!

Jesus told his disciples when He sent them out to preach, that their Heavenly Father would watch over them and they were never to be afraid because God knew and saw everything.

In those days two little sparrows were sold for a penny, but if one of them died He knew about it! He said we are worth so much more than the sparrows to Him! It's very reassuring to know that God is watching over us constantly because we mean so much to Him.

---

### Matthew 10 verses 29 & 31

*Are not two sparrows sold for a penny? Yet not one of them will fall to the ground apart from the will of your Father."*
*"...so don't be afraid; you are worth more than many sparrows."*

# *Sherbet Crystals*

In the sweet shop there was usually a jar on the shelf with layers of multi coloured sherbet crystals. With our pocket money we could go and buy a little cone-shaped bag full of these and we used to dip our finger into the bag and suck the crystals off our finger.

Our parents didn't really approve of these because they were very bad for our teeth, so told us not to buy them.

The problem was that we liked them and brought them anyway – but we always got caught out because the colouring stained our finger!

Sadly, our lives have been 'stained' by sin, but God has made provision for those 'stains' to be removed and for us to be clean and acceptable to Him.

### Isaiah 1 verse 18

*"Come now, let us reason together, says the Lord. "Though your sins are like scarlet, they shall be as white as snow, though they are red as crimson, they shall be like wool."*

# Murray Mints

Can you remember the little advertisement on TV for these sweets? They used to show someone sat taking their time over eating the sweet when they should have been doing something else!

The words of the jingle were "murray mints, murray mints, too good to hurry mints"!

These days life is one big rush and hurry. We would do well sometimes to just stop and sit and enjoy some of the sweet things God has given us – our gardens, a beautiful view, a lovely sunset.

We miss so many lovely times by always being in a hurry – so relax!

**Matthew 11 verse 28**

*"Come to me all you who are weary and burdened, and I will give you rest."*

# *Love Hearts*

A packet of Love Hearts always gave us some fun as children. Apart from being nice fizzy sweets, they each had a message on them and we would give them to the boys we liked at school!

God sends us messages of love through His Word, the Bible and these words of love are always there to reassure us, not like the little messages on the sweets which dissolved immediately you put them into your mouth.

God's love for us lasts forever and will never change.

**Jeremiah 31 verse 3**

*"…I have loved you with an everlasting love;
I have drawn you with loving-kindness."*

# *Pear Drops*

Pear Drops are pleasant sweets to suck, but don't really taste like pears! They are probably called that because they are made in the shape of a pear.

Like all fruits, pears are good for us. My neighbour has a pear tree and it's fascinating to watch them growing week by week from tiny little dots, to large juicy refreshing fruits.

We don't know how this miracle happens, but it does, and we can benefit.

In life we don't need to know how everything comes about, but we need to accept that we have a great Creator who provides all our needs for the whole of our lives. Let's thank Him today for the miracles of nature.

---

### Genesis 2 verse 9

*"And the Lord God made all kinds of trees grow out of the ground – trees that were pleasing to the eye and good for food…"*

# Honey & Lemon Drops

Two contrasting tastes in one sweet. Honey being sweet and soothing and lemon being tart and bitter, yet together they work and can bring soothing comfort to a sore throat!

Our lives are a bit like this mixture. We have sweet and enjoyable times, yet mixed in with these are bitter and sad experiences, but together they serve God's purposes for us.

Even Jesus experienced both bitter and sweet in His time on earth. Together these experiences make us the people we are and with God's help we can be useful and a great comfort to others.

---

**Romans 8 verse 28**

*"And we know that in all things God works for the good of those who love Him, who have been called according to His purpose."*

# Jelly Babies

Tiny little coloured jelly sweets shaped like a baby!

They are all identical because they are made in little moulds so that they all come out exactly the same shape.

How amazing to think that each one of us is completely unique. God didn't make us all identical. We each have special features, different characters, talents and skills. But we were each created by God to be His friend – what a privilege!

Best of all He knows every detail about each of us – even how many hairs we have on our heads. That's too much for us to comprehend really, but one thing we can know is that He loves and cares for us as individuals – not just a crowd of human beings, like jelly babies in a sweet jar!

**Psalm 139 verse 14**

*"I praise you because I am fearfully and wonderfully made; your works are wonderful, I know that full well."*

# *Fisherman's Friend*

A sweet with a purpose!

These were used by Fishermen out on the cold seas at night. They had medicinal and warming properties.

Several of Jesus' disciples were fishermen. He called them from their fishing jobs to follow Him, and when they obeyed He became their friend – and what a friend – their lives were changed forever!

When we take Jesus as our friend, He brings healing to our lives and the warmth of a friendship that will last forever. We all need a friend who is always there for us.

---

**Proverbs 18 verse 24**

*"A man of many friends may come to ruin, but there is a Friend who sticks closer than a brother."*

## Rock

A stick of rock is a very fascinating sweet. As children if our friends went to the seaside for a holiday, it was customary for them to bring us back a stick of rock!

It was usually pink in colour and peppermint flavoured, but very hard – hence the name!

The thing that always baffled me, was how the name of the seaside town they'd been to, was printed in the rock and remained there till I had eaten right down to the bottom!

It's amazing to think that God's Word (written for us in the Bible) has endured for so long and will remain until the end of time as we know it. It doesn't change even though men try to water it down or disprove it. We can rely on it. It is like a 'rock' in our lives if we read and apply it – a safe place, a firm foundation.

**Isaiah 26 verse 4**

*"Trust in the Lord forever,
for the Lord, the Lord,
is the Rock eternal."*

# *Chocolate Coins*

These usually come out at Christmas as a stocking filler or to hang on the Christmas Tree.

The outside is gold foil and inside is solid creamy chocolate, and children love them. Some adults do too!

Jesus once told a story about a woman who had ten coins, each one probably worth about a day's wages. She lost one in her house and searched frantically until she found it. When she did, she called her friends and neighbours to celebrate.

Did you know, that every time a person turns to God and becomes a Christian, that the angels in heaven celebrate?! How amazing to think that heaven would celebrate that I had become part of God's family. Have you given Heaven something to celebrate?

### Luke 15 verse 10

*"In the same way, I tell you, there is rejoicing in the presence of the angels of God over one sinner who repents."*

# Jelly Dew Drops

What a lovely feeling it is to go out into the garden very early on a spring or summer morning, and see the dew glistening on the grass and flowers. Everything is so fresh and sweet smelling.

These little multi-coloured sweets are like the rainbow colours created by the morning sun on the dew.

As we look around at the beauty of a new day, we are reminded of God's love for us. He has brought us through another night into a new fresh morning and is ready to give us all His blessings for that day!

### Lamentations 3 verse 22-23

*"Because of the Lord's great love we are not consumed, for His compassions never fail. They are new every morning; great is your faithfulness."*

# *Rainbow Drops*

Little chocolate buttons covered in 'hundreds and thousands' – tiny multi-coloured bits of sugar! Hence the name 'Rainbow Drops'

Every time I hear the word rainbow, I think of that beautiful sight we see in the sky after a storm. The multi-coloured bow which reminds us of a promise that God made way back in the days of Noah – and it's still there today – because God's promises remain for ever. He never breaks His promises to us. He is a totally faithful friend.

### Genesis 9 verses 12 & 13

*And God said, "This is the sign of the covenant I am making between me and you and every living creature with you, a covenant for all generations to come: I have set my rainbow in the clouds, and it will be the sign of the covenant between me and the earth."*

# *Gob Stoppers!!*

As a young girl, these sweets always amazed me – they were so big – how could anyone ever get one in their mouth? Yet they did, and it was usually the boys at school! They certainly served a purpose, and kept them quiet for quite a while!

One of the biggest failings in today's society is that there are very few listeners, but an awful lot of talkers! We don't listen nearly enough, to each other or the Lord.

Sometimes it is good to be silent – we would learn so much more!

### Ecclesiastes 3 verse 1 & 7

*"There is a time for everything, and a season for every activity under heaven:*

*"…a time to be silent and a time to speak."*

# *Parma Violets*

At school we often used to carry a little packet of sweets in our school bags called Parma Violets. Tiny little mauve coloured sweets that had a lovely taste and always made our breath smell sweet like violets. After eating them we were surrounded by a pleasant fragrance.

In the Bible Mary, one of Jesus' friends poured expensive perfume on His feet as a token of her devotion and it filled the house with a lovely fragrance.

The presence of Jesus in our lives can be like a 'sweet fragrance' as we show His love to those around us who are looking for hope, encouragement and support in life.

### John 12 verse 3

*"Then Mary took about a pint of pure nard, an expensive perfume; she poured it on Jesus' feet and wiped His feet with her hair. And the house was filled with the fragrance of the perfume.*

**Day 25**

## *Sugared Almonds*

These sweets are often used as 'favours' given to guests at weddings. They are pretty, pale colours and have a sugar shell – but have you ever tried to bite into one?!

They are so hard it takes some time to get through to the lovely almond nut in the middle, but it's worth the effort!

Some folks are like that – quite hard to get to know, but once you get through to the heart of them, they can be great people and good friends. Patience is a great asset when trying to break down hardness, so stick at it if you are trying to help someone.

**1 Corinthians 13 verse 4**

"Love is patient, love is kind…"

# Edinburgh Rock

The name 'rock' for this sweet is a bit misleading really, because although it is hard, the minute you put it in your mouth it begins to melt!

We always associate rock with something solid, reliable, unmoving and safe. Thankfully we have a God who is like that. He is someone on whom we can totally depend. He remains strong when everything else around us fails or collapses.

When King David wrote some of the Psalms, he wrote of the Lord being his 'rock' and his fortress – a safe place to run!

The Lord can be exactly that to us today!

---

**Psalm 18 verses 1-2**

*"I love you, O Lord, my strength. The Lord is my rock, my fortress and my deliverer; my God is my rock, in whom I take refuge..."*

# Glacier Mints

I always think of a polar bear when I see these sweets! The advertisements for Glacier Mints had a polar bear standing on a large clear mint, which looked like an iceberg and you could see right through it! After a few minutes in your mouth, glacier mints do become completely transparent.

Did you know that our lives are 'transparent' before God too?

He sees everything we do, knows every thought we have, and knows every detail about our lives – yet loves us anyway!

That is so reassuring when we realise there are things we are ashamed of yet He is willing to forgive.

### Psalm 139 verses 1-3

*"O Lord, you have searched me and you know me. You know when I sit and when I rise, you perceive my thoughts from afar. You discern my going out and my lying down; You are familiar with all my ways."*

## *Refreshers*

These are round sherbet sweets with a real 'zing' when you put them in your mouth. They leave a lovely fresh taste and come in various fruit flavours.

Have you ever invited someone to your home who was tired, weary and downhearted? Perhaps you gave them some rest, some company and a nice drink and later they went away 'refreshed'.

It's always good to have nice things done for us when we're tired, discouraged and in need of some tender loving care.

Did you know that the Bible says if we are generous with our time, possessions and hospitality, we too will be blessed?!

**Proverbs 11 verse 25**

*"A generous man will prosper; he who refreshes others will himself be refreshed."*

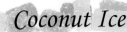

# *Coconut Ice*

If you like coconut, this would probably be among your favourite sweets!

It's made of coconut, milk and sugar and is very sweet indeed. A coconut has many uses and one is that it provides a refreshing drink – coconut milk.

If we belong to the Lord, one thing we need to do is 'grow' as Christians. Like newborn babies need milk to grow, so we need 'spiritual milk'.

Our source of 'spiritual milk' or 'food' is the Bible which contains what we need to know about the Lord, so that we can grow into mature Christians, able to help others.

**1 Peter 2 verses 2 & 3**

*"Like newborn babies, crave spiritual milk, so that by it you may grow up in your salvation, now that you have tasted that the Lord is good."*

# Turkish Delight

We are probably all familiar with this sweet soft rose flavoured confection, which actually did originate in Turkey.

One story is told that Turkish Delights were wrapped in lace hankies and given as a 'chic' gift amongst Socialites and that couples exchanged them as tokens of love.

The word 'delight' indicates 'a source of great joy' God 'delights' in us, He loves us very much, but a good relationship is always a two-way thing – we also need to take delight in the Lord and we will be blessed!

**Psalm 37 verse 4**

*"Delight yourself in the Lord and He will give you the desires of your heart"*

# *Alphabet Letters*

These little crunchy sweets made in the shape of letters of the Alphabet were good fun to have. We could spell out our names and make up messages for our friends with them – depending on how many different letters we had in the bag!

The problem was, they were so nice to eat that they didn't last long – we even had fun eating them – in alphabetical order!

In the Bible we read that God is the 'beginning' and the 'end'. The Alpha and Omega. Alpha is the first letter of the Greek Alphabet and Omega the last.

He rules as sovereign over all human history. He has always been there, is there now, and will be there for ever. That is very reassuring!

### Revelation 1 verse 8

*"I am the Alpha and the Omega" says the Lord God, "who is, and who was, and who is to come, the Almighty."*

# About The Author

Cynthia Huddleston (known as 'Ben') was born in Bath and now lives in North Somerset with her Husband Richard.

Brought up in a Christian home, she is the eldest of five children and became a committed Christian at 13 years old.

Her career was as an Executive PA and Office Manager.

She has been involved with a number of Christian organisations over the years including working for Billy Graham on the Mission England Team in Bristol and Christian Television Association (CTA). In 1997 she and her husband went to East Africa as Missionaries with Mission Aviation Fellowship (MAF).

She studied at Capernwray Bible School, Lancashire and has been a Ladies Speaker for over 10 years.